Forever Friends

A TRUE STORY

KAROL BARKLEY and **D. G. SMEALL**

Illustrated by
SHERRY BENIC

ISBN 978-1-63525-545-4 (Paperback)
ISBN 978-1-63525-546-1 (Digital)

Copyright © 2017 by Karol Barkley and D. G. Smeall
All rights reserved. No part of this publication may be reproduced, distributed, or transmitted in any form or by any means, including photocopying, recording, or other electronic or mechanical methods without the prior written permission of the publisher. For permission requests, solicit the publisher via the address below.

Christian Faith Publishing, Inc.
296 Chestnut Street
Meadville, PA 16335
www.christianfaithpublishing.com

Some illustrations were taken from online clip art and were documented accordingly.

Printed in the United States of America

To all the children

Dedicated to all the children of the world, especially those who have suffered hardship and to the memory of Karol's wonderful father and mother.

Also dedicated, posthumously, to Mr. William Steig, famed cartoonist, renowned children's author, the originator of the Pearl cartoon character and whose influence precipitated the Poor Pitiful Pearl doll. In later years, he was also the creator of the children's story, *Shrek*. Without Mr. Steig's imagination and creativity, Pearl would never have been "born," and the concept for the start of a wonderful community service organization, Toy Rescue Mission[1], benefiting thousands of children and seniors might never have been realized. Mr. Steig passed away in October 2003, but we want to recognize his contributions and part in the creation of one of the main characters of this book. (Our thanks to Mr. Steig for nurturing the child within!)

We also wish to recognize and thank Nikita Lipatov, "adopted son" of Tim and Karol Barkley, for his untiring patience and excellent graphic editing assistance that helped ensure that the illustrations, photos, and clipart included were all digitally correct and ready for publication.

---

[1]. Toy Rescue Mission (TRM) is a nonprofit community service organization. For more information visit the website: www.toyrescuemission.org.

A gem cannot be polished without friction, nor a man perfected without trials.

–Lucius Annaeus Seneca

Peridot

(Pronounced pear-e-dot or pear-e-dough)

Peridot gem designed using MS Paint program

A Note to Parents

Although some of the content contained herein may seem heavy for a children's book, the story is, nonetheless true. The story's heartwarming conclusion justifies the weight of the subject matter, demonstrating that indeed, good can come from difficult life situations if God is in control![2]

The character, Downhearted Dot, is based on a doll that originated from the 1950s, initially as a *derivative work* based on a cartoon character created by *The New Yorker* magazine cartoonist, William Steig. The doll, Poor Pitiful Pearl, was first manufactured by Brookglad Toy Company then later by Horsman Toy Company. Sears, Roebuck and Company[3] sold the doll in their Holiday Catalog beginning in the late 1950s.

Without Pearl's presence in the life of coauthor, Karol Barkley (identified by her Hawaiian name, Nani, in our story), the nonprofit organization, Toy Rescue Mission, would probably not have been created.

Karol founded Toy Rescue Mission in 1991, "to refurbish and recycle gently-used toys for disadvantaged children and seniors in care facilities while providing meaningful volunteer opportunities for the young-at-heart."[4] In so doing, Karol honors the memory of her loving father while providing toys for disadvantaged children to cherish, much like she cherishes her Poor Pitiful Pearl doll even today.

---

[2] Loosely quoted Scripture verse taken from Romans 8:28, "And we know that all things work together for good to them that love God, to them who are the called according to His purpose" (KJV).

[3] All references in the text to Sears, Roebuck and Company are by permission of the company.

[4] TRM Mission Statement.

Toys, though not a basic (or "critical") life need, like food and shelter, are the *TOOLS* children need to carry out their all-important task of playing. The act of playing is as important to a child's emotional and mental development as food and shelter are to their physical well being.[5]

TRM is a nonprofit organization (EIN 91-1629854) under IRS Code 501(c)(3) and is a registered charity with the Secretary of (Washington) State, Corporations Division. To share in this worthwhile project or to find out how you can be involved in volunteer opportunities with Toy Rescue Mission, *no matter where you live*, visit the TRM website: www.toyrescuemission.org and click on the Donations link All donations to TRM are tax-deductible.

If you have comments or questions about this book, you may contact the authors as listed below:

Nani Karol Barkley: toyresq21@gmail.com
Phone: 253-565-6201
Donna Gates-Smeall: dgsmeall@me.com

[5.] Quote from TRM Brochure.

Toy Rescue Mission
607 S. Winnifred St.
Tacoma, WA 98465
253-460-6711
Mailing address: PO Box 64547
Tacoma, WA 98465-0547

Chapter 1

NANI INTRODUCES DOT

My name is Karol, but I am known to those in Hawaii by my Hawaiian name "NANI". This is my story and the story of my Forever Friends.

Before I came to know her, Dot spent her days sitting patiently and quietly on the Sears Roebuck warehouse shelf thousands of miles away from me, swinging her legs and humming her favorite holiday carol, "Joy to the World"[6] along with the music playing on the store's overhead speaker. She still had faith that this year would be *her* special year.

She had been waiting so patiently for several years, waiting to be loved by someone who could look past her tattered appearance and see the love she held in her little doll heart for her Forever Friend.

Most of her prettier doll sisters had already found homes in other parts of the world—all but Dot and one last porcelain doll. Often Dot would comfort herself with the thought that she, too, may soon have a Forever Friend to love. She often wondered where in the world *she* would end up living.

Dot, why even her nickname sounded plain and ordinary! It didn't seem to matter that her *real* name was Peridot, for the beautiful green gemstone necklace that was her one and only possession. She was conscious of the fact that the necklace looked out of

---

[6]. "Joy to the World" is a popular Christmas song. Lyrics written in 1719 by English hymn writer, Isaac Watts; Lowell Mason adapted and arranged the music to Watts' lyrics in 1839.

place with her tatters and patches, but it was the one gift her the Creator had given her to share with her special Forever Friend.

"Joy to the World! The Lord has come; Let earth receive her King; Let every heart prepare Him room . . ." Dot knew the words to this familiar carol by heart and sang it softly to herself, but all the while, her little doll heart ached as she wondered, "Would *this* Christmas be the one when someone would have room in their heart for *me*?"

Chapter 2

NANI'S ISLAND LIFE

Meanwhile thousands of miles away and across the vast Pacific Ocean, I was involved in the day-to-day events of my own life.

I was born and raised in Hawaii, on the island of Oahu. My family consisted of my Mama, Daddy, Aunty Jean, and Uncle Gene. I was an only child, but I had all kinds of *ohana* (family or extended family and close friends) that loved me, along with my ever-faithful companion, a weenie dog named Frisky. Although I was a *haole* (white person), I was also a *kamaaina keiki* (native-born child) with a love and appreciation for my island home.

Day to day, we lived the island life, getting up in the morning, sharing an early breakfast, and preparing for work and school. Mama loved to serve papaya as part of a healthy breakfast, so it was my job to *shinny* up the papaya tree in our backyard and pick her a nice, fresh one! "Catch!" I hollered as I peered down at my mother through the papaya tree leaves. Swiftly, Mama stepped forward to gather up the papaya in her cupped hands.

Papaya illustration from Clipartpanda.com

"Wow!" Mama exclaimed, "that was close. I almost dropped it!" I giggled as I began my downward slide to the ground, stopping momentarily to snap off one of the big leaves; they made the best pea shooters! Nimble and quick, I landed at the bottom of the tree without mishap.

Since we lived across the street from the beach, each day after breakfast, Mama, Daddy, and I would race to see who could get to the water's edge first. Usually I won, probably because I was barefoot and Mama and Daddy were ready for work and had to wear shoes. We spent the next half hour or so searching the water's edge for glass balls, floats that worked their way loose from Japanese fishermen's nets thousands of miles away in Japan. Most of the time, we turned up empty-handed, but once in a while, after a storm, we got lucky and found a few! Then all too soon, it was time to head off to work and school.

I loved my island life! I enjoyed school and was entrenched in local Hawaiian culture. I learned to dance *hula* (Hawaiian dance) from the age of three and was part of a local *halau* (Hawaiian dance troupe). I loved sharing secrets with my *aikane* (friends) and playing at Kalama Beach every day after school—swimming and body surfing in the warm island waters, building sand castles, and sharing old Hawaiian legends with my friends. I loved the feel of the warm sand sifting between my toes, the salty taste of the ocean spray on my tongue, and the breezes blowing through my hair. Often I would stop on my way to and from school, just to inhale the fragrance of the sweet-smelling flowers that grew alongside the roads—plumeria, ginger, gardenia, tuberose, and *so many more!* My favorite was the crown flower bush, with its waxy blossoms and centers that resembled a miniature crown! They made beautiful *lei* (flower wreaths), and the bush was a favorite of the Monarch butterflies that flocked to it. I would often find their chrysalis hanging on the leaves and would break off the branch and place it in a jar by my bed to watch the butterfly emerge.

But most of all, I loved my island foods! I had been raised on a diet of *poi* (starchy food made from the taro plant) and had been known as a *poi* baby growing up. Other favorites were sushi, *saimin, haupia, lomi lomi salmon, chicken long rice, lau lau, manapua,* and *malasadas,* not to mention the vast variety of tropical fruit fresh for the picking such as *lilikoi, guava,* Chinese bananas*, mountain apples, grapefruit, lichee,* and of course, *the morning papaya!*

Crown flower illustration courtesy of Bing original file, jpeg[8]

---

7. See *"Glossary of Hawaiian (and Other) Words"* in the back of the book.
8. Commons, wikimedia.org.

Chapter 3

CHRISTMAS WISHES

One day when I was ten, Daddy came into the family room where Mama and I were watching TV. He was holding the *Sears, Roebuck, and Company Christmas Catalog*. We knew how much he hated to go shopping, so that was his way out! "Ladies, it's time for you two to pick out something special for Christmas." It was only August, but we knew it always took the big cargo ships a long time to bring the packages all the way from the mainland. I eagerly took the catalog and started leafing through its shiny pages in search of my *perfect* gift.

Over the next week, I spent many hours carefully studying the catalog pages, excited at the prospect of being able to pick out my own present! In the past, Mama and Daddy had picked out my presents, so that was truly a special Christmas! I especially loved dolls and had a collection of storybook dolls all neatly displayed in their beautiful costumes on a special shelf Daddy had made just for them! What to choose, a beautiful bride doll or maybe a doll from Scotland, dressed in a kilt?

One Saturday morning, as I was lying on the end of my bed staring at the now-crumpled catalog pages for the *umpteenth* time, I was surprised to find a doll I hadn't noticed before! It was a doll with such bright green eyes they seemed to come alive!

The catalog said her name was Downhearted Dot, and it suited her perfectly, for she certainly wasn't the prettiest or the best-dressed doll; no, not by any means. From her tattered and patched new-old-looking dress to the little matching green polka-dot scarf covering her straight blonde hair, she looked downhearted indeed! But all I could see was a lonely little doll pleading for a home and someone to love her! She needed a friend, and so it was at that moment I knew without a doubt what I wanted for Christmas. Dot, I decided, needed a home and a Forever Friend to love her!

FOREVER FRIENDS

Later that evening, I proudly held up the picture of Dot I had torn out of the catalog and told Mama and Daddy, "I *finally* found what I want for Christmas!" I could see their disappointment in my choice.

"Well, that doll certainly lives up to her name . . . she truly *does* look downhearted and sad!" Mama said. "Why do you want *that* one when there are so many *really pretty* dolls to choose from?" she asked.

"Oh, Mama, you grownups, you just don't understand! Can't you tell by the look in her eyes that she wants me to *hanai* (adopt) her?" There definitely was a look in Dot's sad eyes that went straight to my heart and made me want to adopt her above all others.

Chapter 4

CHRISTMAS DREAMS

After what seemed like forever, December finally arrived, but of course, in Hawaii it's hard to tell. It is not cold and there is no snow! My friends and I still played happily outside in the warm Hawaiian sun. Sometimes though when Mama received Christmas cards from the mainland showing pictures of drifting snow and cozy warm fireplaces, I longed to experience the joys of a real winter, build a snowman, have snowball fights, or even own a coat! I could just imagine a warm fur hood surrounding my face on a snowy winter day!

Our island winters were sunny and warm; the temperature, a balmy eighty degrees outside. With Christmas drawing near, the Outdoor Circle group was holding its annual Outdoor Decorating Contest, and everyone in Kailua town was working hard to set their yards aglow with colorful decorations and Christmas lights! It was so important that we decorate; otherwise who could tell it was actually Christmas?

As Christmas day drew closer, the thought of Dot was with me every day. I would lie awake in bed at night, drifting off to sleep with the sound of the wind rustling in the coconut trees outside my bedroom window and dreaming of Christmas morning and the precious doll I hoped was being packed for delivery just for me!

My friends were all talking about what they wanted for Christmas, but I didn't want to tell them about Dot, just in case Daddy might still decide to surprise me with a pretty storybook doll instead.

What I didn't know was that Daddy had seen the longing in my eyes and understood my wish to adopt the one special doll, so to be sure she arrived in time, he had placed the order in the mail just after my birthday back in August.

He, too, was excited! Little did I know that he couldn't *wait* to see the look on my face when I opened the box on Christmas morning! He knew that Downhearted Dot was probably already on her way to Hawaii along with a special dress for Mama.

Chapter 5

MELE KALIKIMAKA PARTY

Two weeks before Christmas, Mama and I were busy with the preparations and planning of my *Mele Kalikimaka* (Merry Christmas) Party. Every year, Mama and I planned the holiday event, and it had become my special Christmas tradition. I made a list and invited all my *aikane* (friends) and *ohana*—friends, neighbors, and extended family. They knew to wear their best island clothes: *muu muu* (Hawaiian loose-fitting dress), *holomuu* (a muu muu fitted at the waist), *holokuu* (a holomuu with a long train), *aloha* (Hawaiian print) shirts, *slippas* (slippers, flip flops) or just their bare feet! I spent hours planning the afternoon's activities. We would play *konane* (a Hawaiian game similar to checkers, but played with pieces of lava rock, shells, and coral), weave *lauhala* (leaves from the hala tree) leaf placemats for Christmas gifts, make *kapa*[9] (Hawaiian fabric made from the paper-bark tree) decorations from paper grocery bags, sing traditional Hawaiian Christmas *meles* (songs), and of course, eat lots of *ono* (delicious) food!

[9.] See instructions for homemade *kapa* in back of book.

"So what are we having for *kau kau* (food)?" I asked Mama one day shortly before the party.

"Oh, *Nani*," (Mama and my friends often called me by my Hawaiian nickname), "we're having your favorites: *lomi lomi* (raw salmon) and *poi* (see glossary), *Tutu's Pupus* (Gramma's snacks), *haupia* (coconut pudding), and *lilikoi* (passion fruit juice)."

"*Aue*, Mama, don't forget the *crack seed*!" (dried fruit treats) I laughed as my mouth watered at the thought of my favorite island treat! "Can we make some *lei* (flower wreaths) too?" (A Hawaiian tradition is to give lei along with a kiss when greeting guests on special occasions.)

"Of course, Nani," Mama agreed, "and Aunty Jean says you can pick the plumeria flowers for your friends' lei from her tree."

Chapter 6

AN UNEXPECTED HOSPITAL VISIT

It had finally arrived, December 13th, the day of my Mele Kalikimaka party! Excitedly I threw off my covers and fairly flew out of bed as I ran in search of Mama. Passing through the family room, I noticed Daddy stretched out in his favorite *papa-san* (recliner-type chair), looking like he wasn't feeling too well. While I hurried to eat breakfast and get dressed, Mama also noticed that Daddy didn't look well and was insisting that he go to the doctor. Daddy rarely got sick, and he certainly didn't like the fuss Mama was making, but he finally agreed to go. I, of course, was so busy with my party preparations that I didn't even notice he was gone.

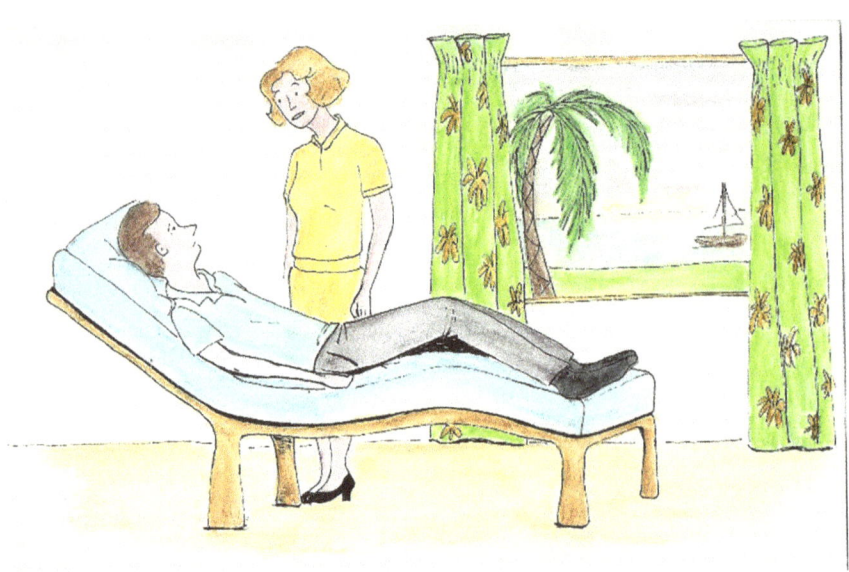

By evening, my party was over, but it had been a huge success with games, prizes, and lots of food and fun! As we cleaned up the mess, Mama seemed troubled and said, "Dr. Akaka told Daddy today that he had to go into Honolulu to Queen's Hospital to get some rest and have some tests done."

Rarely ever had I seen my Daddy sick; worriedly I asked, "How long will he be there? Do you think he'll be home in time for Christmas, Mama?" I couldn't imagine our Christmas with Daddy lying in a hospital bed.

"Yes, I think so. He wants very much to be here to celebrate with us," Mama said, trying to hide her own fears. She added, "We're going over to pick up Aunty Jean and Uncle Gene so we can all go to the hospital to visit him." Uncle Gene and I were especially close, so I was comforted in knowing he would be there.

Chapter 7

KEEPING PROMISES

Later that same evening, as he was laying in his hospital bed, Daddy began to sense that he wasn't getting any better. He wasn't sure what was wrong, but he knew it wasn't good. After talking with the doctors, he soon realized how sick he really was and that he might *not* be coming home in time for Christmas. Daddy sent the rest of us out of the room for a few minutes so he could talk to Uncle Gene and share a secret about the special presents he had ordered from the catalog and hidden in the *pune'e* (sofa bed) back at home.

"Would you please, make sure Nani and Mama get their gifts on Christmas Day? I want them to know that I will love them always, no matter what happens," he whispered. Uncle Gene knew Daddy was getting weaker, but he tried to hide his concern, so he sadly agreed to carry out his wishes. Mama and Aunty Jean stepped back into the hospital room just in time to hear Daddy whisper, "I love you!" to Mama, and "Tell Nani I love her!" and then he slowly closed his eyes.

I was standing alone in the hallway as the three of them came out of the hospital room with their heads bowed and tears flowing freely. Above the background of the hospital noises, I could hear the soft, sweet words of "Silent Night"[10] as it echoed in the hallway, when they broke the news that my Daddy had died!

---

[10]. "Silent Night", a popular Christmas carol composed in 1818 by Franz Xaver Gruber to lyrics by Joseph Mohr

Chapter 8

UNEXPECTED SURPRISES!

The remaining days before Christmas passed in a blur. There was scarcely a thought about celebrations or presents. The Christmas morning dawned bright and warm but felt gray with sadness in our house without Daddy. Mama and I sat on the *pune'e* (day bed) hugging each other as we stared with tired, tear-filled eyes at the bubble lights on the Christmas tree.

In the silence between us, there came a knock on the screen door. There stood Uncle Gene and Aunty Jean, singing *Mele Kalikimaka* (Hawaiian Christmas carol). After our usual round of hugs, Uncle Gene said, "I have a surprise for both of you!" as he walked over to the *pune'e* where we were sitting, bent down, and gently pulled from underneath it two carefully wrapped packages. "Your Daddy wanted you both to know how much he loved you," Uncle Gene said as he handed presents to each of us. "He asked me to wrap these special gifts he bought and keep them as a surprise for you till Christmas morning." My hands shook as I reached out to take the box Uncle Gene offered. Through my tears, I read the attached gift card, "To my precious Nani, with love from Daddy."

As I carefully unwrapped and opened the box, wonder and tears filled my eyes as I whispered, "Dot, I got my Downhearted Dot! Daddy didn't forget how much I wanted her!" I hugged Dot tightly, and I was sure that Dot, with her tiny doll-arms, was hugging me back. I found great comfort holding Dot close, and I felt certain as I looked into her green eyes that *her* life was complete, having a special little girl to love her.

"Oh, my!" was all Mama could say, choking back her own tears as she opened her box and saw the beautiful new dress before her. Daddy had ordered the exact one she had chosen from the catalog! Mama and I held tightly to the gifts Daddy had left for us. That Christmas morning, our sadness was softened by the sweet memories of a loving daddy and husband.

Chapter 9

PERIDOTS

It isn't hard to imagine how difficult that Christmas was for us. But time had a way of passing and healing some of the hurting. As the years passed, Dot could still be found sitting proudly in her special place on my bed, watching as I was growing up. She had come to me wearing one prized possession, a beautiful green peridot necklace that matched her eyes! I knew she was more than willing to share the necklace with me, and I wore it often.

What made it even *more* special was that the stone was actually the birthstone for the month of August, my birthstone! I studied to find out more about peridots and learned that most of them are found in the state of Arizona, but I was surprised to find that Hawaii's volcanoes also produce peridots! In the Hawaiian Islands, they're known as *Pele's Tears*, named after the legendary fire goddess, *Madame Pele*. When I looked at my necklace, it reminded me of Green Sand Beach on the Big Island of Hawaii with its tiny grains of peridot sand. Even as I grew older, these memories made me treasure this special gift from Dot, and I wore my necklace proudly to remind me of my home, my doll, and my daddy's unconditional love.

www.photos-public-domain.com/catagoryobjectsjewelry.jpg

Chapter 10

ANOTHER BIG TURN

In the two years following Daddy's death, things grew even more difficult, and my life took another big turn. Mama and I were both so lonely without Daddy, but as weeks turned into months, Mama didn't seem to get any better. She was not only sad and lonely, but often sick, and I didn't know why. As the weeks passed, she seemed to grow weaker until finally, she too had go to Queen's Hospital. After a long stay there, the sad day came when Uncle Gene held me in his arms as he shared, "Your precious Mama has gone to Heaven."

Without my Mama and Daddy, I was then an orphan. Uncle Gene took me aside, saying, "Honey, I wish we could keep you with us, but unfortunately, that's not possible. You will be going to live on the mainland with your grandparents in Tacoma, Washington." My heart broke as I thought of all I had to leave behind, my island lifestyle, my friends, and especially all the people I dearly loved!

After spending the next few weeks with friends, Uncle Gene and I went back to my house. Everything looked the same, but of course, it wasn't the same without my parents there to make it come alive. Uncle Gene explained, "You will have to go through the house and choose the things you want to take with you to the mainland, but," he cautioned, "you can only take what can fit inside a shipping crate the size of a piano." I looked around my home, Mama and Daddy's bedroom, the living room, the family room, my bedroom, and the kitchen. *That was impossible!* There were so many things that reminded me of my precious mama and daddy. How could I ever choose? But choose I must, so I picked out the things that meant the most to a thirteen-year-old girl.

Scooping up my precious Frisky dog and burying my face in his fur to hide my tears, I stated to no one in particular, "No question about it, you and Downhearted Dot will be going to Gramma and Grampa's, and you won't be riding in any old shipping crate! Nope, you'll both go with me right onto the plane!" Then Uncle Gene picked out some things that he knew would be important to me when I grew up, and he put those things away at his house for safekeeping.

The sad day came too soon when I finally had to say my *alohas* (good-byes). Hugs and kisses came from all those who had come to the airport to see me leave. When I finally boarded the plane, I had so many lei around my neck that they reached up to my chin!

Clipart airplane-courtesy of HD Wallpapers-martinea.biz

As the plane taxied down the runway, I buried my face in their sweet fragrance so I didn't have to look out the window and see everyone waving their good-byes. Then began the long trip to Tacoma, where a new chapter of my life was about to begin with Gramma and Grampa Obie waiting to make a new home for me.

Aloha clipart courtesy of Hawaiian Aloha Clip Art Free Flowerclipart.com

Chapter 11

TACOMA

My life in Tacoma was far different from my island life. Gone were all the people I had known and loved, the warm island sun that shone all year round, the sandy beach and ocean across the street from my house plus my favorite island foods, and all the island culture I loved so much. Gramma insisted I be called by my given name, Karol, instead of Nani. I had never known a real winter where it was cold, and although I used to dream of white Christmases, Washington State was more rain than snow! I had never before owned a coat, but that time I not only owned one, I needed to *wear* one! I complained about having to wear shoes all the time! I had been used to going barefoot or just wearing *slippas* (flip flops). Sometimes I would get so homesick, I would cry and beg to go back home, but I knew in my heart that Tacoma was where Frisky, Dot, and I would have to stay.

Just a few months after my arrival, I awoke to a new sight. Everything outside my bedroom window was all white! "Oh, my gosh, it's snowing!" I squealed in delight as I jumped into my shoes without any socks, found my coat, and threw it on over my PJs. I had never seen *real* snow, just pictures on Christmas cards!

As I raced out the door, Gramma called out after me, "You'd better put on some socks! You'll catch pneumonia!" (My Gramma thought *everything* would make me catch pneumonia). But my feet soon found out, as did the rest of me, that it was colder than I had imagined! Of course, I had Frisky and Dot, but they didn't appreciate the snow like people did! I couldn't help but laugh though as I watched poor little Frisky try to bite at the unfamiliar stuff falling from the sky and wade through the snow mounds with his short little weenie-dog legs! I stuck out my tongue to catch the flakes, and as much as they fascinated me, I longed to share the new experience with my Mama and Daddy and close friends back home. And even though I delighted in the new experience, it only temporarily softened my homesickness for Hawaii.

Chapter 12

NEW EXPERIENCES—BIBLE CAMP

The next summer after I moved to the mainland, Gramma told me she was sending me to a girls' Bible camp for a week. Bible Camp, I had never been to a Bible camp before and certainly didn't want to go to one then! "I won't know anyone there," I moaned, "and I certainly don't want to sit around in some stuffy old building praying and reading the Bible all day!" But Gramma knew best, and when she made up her mind, there was no changing it!

Bible illustration courtesy of Bing clip art, Public Domain Bible

When we arrived, I found that the camp was built right next to the ocean on Puget Sound, so immediately, that made things more acceptable! I hadn't seen the ocean in the year since I'd moved to Washington because unlike my home in Hawaii that was located across the street from the beach, the *real* ocean (not Puget Sound, but the Pacific Ocean) was two hours away from Tacoma! There was no stopping me. I rushed to the water's edge and waded right in, but boy was that a shock! Instead of the warm Pacific Ocean I had been accustomed to, *that* ocean (Puget Sound) was cold and *gray*! I hurried out of the ice-cold water onto the hard sand and found a rock to plunk down on so I could try to figure out how the same ocean could be both warm and turquoise blue in Hawaii but cold and gray there in Washington.

My thoughts were interrupted by the sound of laughter and squeals nearby, so I set off to see where all the noise was coming from. To my amazement, there were lots of other girls my age piling out of cars, and most seemed really excited to be there! Some were outgoing but seemed new to the Bible Camp stuff, just like I was.

We were quickly assigned to counselors who led the way to our cabins. I was in the process of testing the lumps in the mattress of my lower bunk when I heard a friendly, "Hi, there!" come from up above me. Ginny, a girl with curly blonde hair peered down with a welcoming grin. She seemed very outgoing and friendly. As we unpacked and were getting settled, we had time to get acquainted and quickly found we had much in common. She had brought her favorite friend with her, a limp and lumpy stuffed puppy she called Max. Of course, my Dot was safely snuggled down in my sleeping bag out of sight because I was fourteen and almost a grown up!

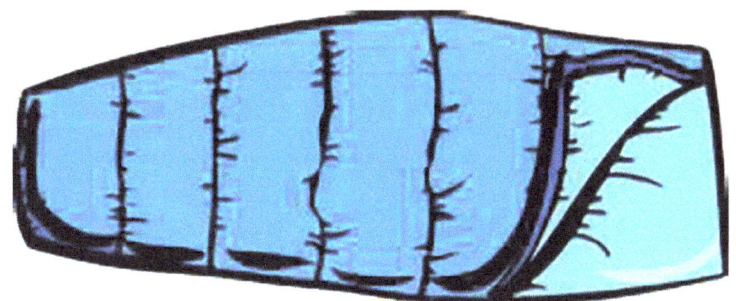

Sleeping bag clip art courtesy of free-illustrations.gatag.net

Each afternoon after free time, there was an hour when all the girls could choose between going to the gym for a time of prayer or just hang out and have more free time. Back home in Hawaii, I had always gone to church with Mama but had never spent much time praying, mostly just the usual grace at meals and a bedtime prayer. Ginny and I quickly decided that the prayer stuff just wasn't what we had in mind. By midweek though, we were getting a bit bored with our extra free time. We had caught our share of fish, played plenty of basketball, gone to the beach (brrrrr), but then what to do? We decided to find out more about the prayer time some of our fellow campmates were attending, so we quietly tiptoed into the back of the gym to see for ourselves what it was all about. To our surprise, there were other girls our age kneeling there with the camp counselors, earnestly praying for the week's activities and for all the girls attending the camp! No one was forcing them to be there! Ginny and I didn't quite know what to make of that and quietly slipped back out the door, hoping no one had seen us.

Girl Praying—Bing image, general domain

Chapter 13

BORN AGAIN?

After that uncomfortable hour was over, we were required to attend the evening meeting with singing and a message from a guest speaker. As the singing began, Ginny and I filed into the big chapel along with all the other camp girls. A lady up front was turning pages on a big paper tablet that contained the words of the songs they were singing. As I started to sing along, the words seemed to jump off the pages and right into my heart! They spoke about how God wanted to take away all of my sadness and hurt, about how much he loved us, cared about what happens to us, and how he wanted to bring us real joy and happiness! I began to realize that the *us* we were singing about really included me!

As the missionary lady spoke about God wanting to be a loving Father to us, I thought about how much I missed my real daddy and mama. *Oh, how I wanted a father!* I couldn't believe what I was hearing! All I had to do was accept his love in the gift of his Son, Jesus and ask him to come into my heart.

As the missionary speaker continued, I found myself hanging on her every word. She shared about the people she had lived with in faraway Tanganyika (now Tanzania) and how she had taken the Bible, the Word of God, to those who needed him so much. She explained to them about sin, how all people *everywhere* sin, how doing bad things like telling lies, disobeying, and taking things that don't belong to them were just some of the ways we can sin, and how our sin can come between us and a loving heavenly

Father. But then she explained how those people, like the girls at our camp, could pray and tell Jesus about their own sin, how Jesus had died on a cross to take all sin away if they would only accept his gift—the new life he was offering them! I soon realized that I was no different from the people in Tanganyika. I told lies, and I had even taken things that didn't belong to me, which I knew was stealing. That meant that I, too, needed Jesus's gift of forgiveness.

Then I remembered Downhearted Dot snuggled down in my sleeping bag back in the cabin. I knew how much I loved her! What if I hadn't accepted the gift from my loving daddy? I wouldn't have Dot in my life that day! I knew at that moment that I needed to accept God's gift and ask Jesus into my life right then and there! I didn't even hesitate, and as I stood up, I saw Ginny standing, too, ready to make that same decision! As the missionary was asking who wanted to come up and talk with her about those things, Ginny and I almost tripped over each other trying to get to the front of the chapel!

Cross illustration courtesy of Biblical Easter Coloring Pages: Public Domain, http://www.shirleys-preschool-activities.com/

Chapter 14

A LOVING FATHER

In the days, weeks, and months that followed, I never forgot the decision I had made that day at camp. I found that I did have a new life in Jesus! Did that bring back my mama and daddy? Did that mean I got to go back home to Hawaii? No, that wasn't part of God's plan for my new life. But it did mean that I now wanted to live to please Jesus, and someday I would have a new home in heaven with him!

He had come to comfort me as he promised to be a Father to me and bring new joy into my life. Did I sometimes still feel sad and sometimes do bad things, tell a lie, or worse, sin? Yes, sadly at times, I did. But Jesus was sharing my life, helping me know when I was doing wrong, and he was there to help me make good choices just like my daddy had done for me.

When I had first gone to the Bible camp, I couldn't imagine praying. Then I liked to pray because it was a way I could talk to God. Prayer became a part of my daily life. As I lay in bed at night with Frisky snuggled at my feet under the covers, I imagined God holding me close to him, just as I was holding my precious Dot!

I had also learned at camp that talking to God isn't just a one-way conversation. He wants to talk to us through his Word, the Bible. All we have to do is read it!

Bible illustration courtesy of Bible Clip Art, Cartoon Drawings.net, public domain

Chapter 15

ALL GROWN UP!

The years now seemed to be flying by, and the next thing I knew, I was all grown up! I then had a husband, Tim and two little daughters, Brenda and Dayna.

One day I noticed that poor little Dot had gotten older, too! Her patched little dress was in tatters! Worn and ragged even her patches needed patches! I searched high and low and found some scraps of suitable fabric and made Dot another new-old dress. I went through all the local thrift stores to find her some new-old socks and shoes, and then made a new-old polka-dotted green-and-white scarf to cover her faded blonde hair. Holding her at arm's length, I laughed as I said to no one in particular, "Well, I'll be! You look almost like your picture in that old Sears catalog! I wish Daddy could see you now!"

Chapter 16

AN ANNUAL CHRISTMAS TRADITION

Christmas season was upon us again. After much to-do and preparation, it was finally Christmas Eve! Our little family snuggled close by the cozy fireplace as Brenda and Dayna's Daddy once again read the age-old story from the now worn family Bible about the love of our Heavenly Father who sent his Son, Jesus, to be the Savior of the world. We knew the story well. Brenda and Dayna knew it from Sunday school as the nativity story. I then shared with our daughters how Jesus had become my Forever Friend when I accepted his gift of love and salvation! "But, Mama, the story's isn't finished without the last part," begged Brenda and Dayna. Their eyes stared into mine as I shared the love of my wonderful daddy and the special gift he left behind for me, a gift I treasured more with each passing year. As we looked over at Downhearted Dot, sitting close by in her special little rocking chair on the warm fireplace hearth, her still bright green eyes seemed to be taking it all in. It was easy to imagine that we could almost hear her softly humming with us our favorite Christmas carol, "Joy to the World." As the words of the song flowed softly through the room, I suddenly realized that Dot's name no longer fit!

Downhearted, hardly! Though she still wore her patched new-old clothes and new-old shoes, she and I were no longer downhearted at all! We had both accepted the love of a Forever Friend. Dot had found her Forever Friend in me, and I had found my Forever Friend in Jesus and in Dot!

Epilogue

THE REST OF THE STORY

But my story doesn't end there, oh no. As time went by, I began to realize how much joy I had found in my precious Dot and in my Lord Jesus. I found myself wanting to share that joy with other children who weren't as fortunate as I was to have such wonderful gifts. I knew in my community there were children who had no houses to live in and no possessions to call their own. There were children whose parents couldn't afford to buy them Christmas presents or Easter baskets or even a birthday present! My heart ached to have them know that someone cared and wanted to share the joy with them that a Forever Friend can bring. So I founded Toy Rescue Mission, a nonprofit agency dedicated to seeing that those children had their own toys, dolls, stuffed animals, and books to cherish and play with.

Though I am now retired from my work with Toy Rescue Mission, over a span of 20 years, with God's help, I was able to share His Love, and Jesus, my Forever Friend, with the people who came to visit Toy Rescue Mission. Over the years, and with the help and support of thousands of volunteers, Toy Rescue Mission came to be known as a place that connected boys and girls with toys--Forever Friends. By rescuing needy toys, and sharing them with needy children, each one finds a Forever Friend to love, and hopefully, in time these children, and maybe even you, will find, just as I did, their Forever Friend in Jesus!

Jesus is our Forever Friend. "For God loved the world so much that He gave His one and only Son, so that everyone who believes in Him will not perish but have eternal life" (John 3:16 NLT)[11].

Calvary Cross illustration courtesy of Bing Openclipart.org

---

[11] John 3:16 NLT (https://www.blueletterbible.org/)

Story all pau! (finished)

Hawaiian flower clipart borders, freebordersandclipart.com

A Special Offer!

You may not have the same needs as Nani (Karol) in our story, and maybe you don't need toys like the ones given out at Toy Rescue Mission (TRM). At TRM, we have provided many children with gifts and Forever Friends over the years. The gifts were given because we care about those who have a need for them. But those gifts will only be good for a while, and then will eventually become worn out and thrown away. But we also care about you!

If you don't know Jesus as your personal Savior and God as your heavenly Father, then your need is as great as Karol's. We would like to offer you a gift that can't be broken or outgrown and does not need to be refurbished like TRM toys.

It is the Gift of God's love. When God sent his Son Jesus to be the Savior of the world, he gave us the best gift he had to give! If you receive the gift of Jesus, you also receive these other special gifts, all wrapped up in him:

> A Father's love like no other. "As the Father loved me, I also have loved you…Greater love has no one than this, than to lay down one's life for his friends" (John 15:9, 13 NLT).

> Forgiveness for your sin. "If we confess our sins, He is faithful and just and will forgive us our sins and cleanse us from all unrighteousness" (1 John 1:9). You may think you don't need Jesus to save you, but *think again*! If you have ever done even one wrong thing in your whole life, then you have sinned and are in need of Jesus to save you!

Eternal life. "For God so loved the world that he gave his one and only Son, that whosoever believes in him shall not perish but have eternal life" (John 3:16).

Comfort from the Holy Spirit. Jesus promised, "Praise be to . . . the God of all comfort, Who comforts us in all our troubles" (2 Corinthians 1:3).

A home in heaven. Jesus promised, "In my Father's house are many mansions; . . . I go to prepare a place for you" (John 14: 2).

Do you want to receive this gift God has for you? You need only to ask Him for it. **It's as easy as** reaching out and receiving a present, as easy as ABC:

Admit that you're a sinner (see Romans 3:23).

Believe that Jesus is God's Son and is his gift to you (see John 1:12).

Confess (tell God) that you need to receive his gift of forgiveness (see Romans 10:9–10).

Realizing you have a need is one thing but accepting the gift is another. To accept God's gift, simply pray a short prayer like this one:

Lord Jesus, thank you for dying on the cross for my sins, the things I have done that hurt you. I open the door to my life and accept you as my Savior and accept your gift of eternal life. Please guide me—what I do and what I say. Help me to be the kind of person you want me to be. Thank you that you've promised in your Word, the Bible, that you will never leave me! In Jesus's name, amen."

Jesus is both the Gift and the Giver of every good gift! Remember, at Toy Rescue Mission, we give away toys that bring happiness for a time, but only Jesus offers life and joy forever! Please accept God's gift today! If you have more questions about this gift or if you make the choice to ask Jesus to be your Savior, please contact us and let us know! We care and are praying for you!

Nani Karol Barkley: toyresq21@gmail.com or 253-565-6201

Donna Smeall: dgsmeall@me.com

Hawaiian Alphabet

and

BASIC PRONUNCIATION GUIDE

Hibiscus flowers clip art courtesy of http://cliparts.co/tropical-flower-clip-art

A as in "ah"

e as in "eh"

H

I as in *eye*

K

L

M

N

O as in "oh"

P

T (not originally in the Hawaiian language, borrowed from Tahitian language, Hawaiian language usually uses *K* to replace *t*.)

u as in "oo"

W after the letters *i* and *e* the *w* is usually pronounced like *v* after *o* or *u* then it is pronounced like *w* at the beginning of a word or after the letter *a*, it is pronounced either way (*v* or *w*).

Glossary of Hawaiian (and Other) Words

aikane. friend

Aloha. hello (also means good-bye, love)

crack seed. island treats made from dried fruits (plums, cherries, ginger, and mangoes) with licorice, salt, and spice flavorings added. Crack seed is a local island treat! The type shown below is known as Kam Cho Harm Mui.

Crack seed photo courtesy of the Crack Seed Center website; http://www.crackseedcenter.com; Copyright © 2004 Crack Seed Center. All Rights Reserved. Crack Seed Center, 1450 Ala Moana Blvd., #1044, Honolulu, HI 96814

guava. A tropical edible fruit.

halau. Hawaiian dance troupe.

hanai. Raise like a foster child.

haole. White person, Caucasian.

hauole. Happy.

haupia. Coconut finger gelatin (see recipe enclosed).

holokuu. A holokuu with a train.

holomuu. A muu muu fitted at the waist.

hula. Hawaiian dance.

kamaaina. Local islander; native born.

kapa. Hawaiian fabric made from the paper-bark tree.

kau kau. Food (any kind).

keiki. Child.

konane. Hawaiian checkers.

lau lau. Pork and butterfish wrapped in ti leaves and banana leaves and steamed in an underground oven for several hours.

lau hala placemats. Leaves from the *hala* tree, woven into placemats.

lei. Flower wreaths worn around the neck.

lilikoi. Passion fruit.

lomi lomi salmon. Cured in salt raw salmon, combined with diced tomatoes, green onions and water.

long rice. Japanese cellophane noodles.

lychee. Sweet grape-like fruit encased in tough outer skin.

malasada. A Portuguese type of doughnut.

manapua. Chinese pork-filled bun.

Mele Kalikimaka. Merry Christmas.

meles. Songs.

muu muu. Hawaiian loose-fitting dress.

nani. Pretty or beautiful.

ohana. Family or extended family, friends, etc.

ono. Good, yummy!

papasan chair. Long curved chair similar to a futon.

papaya. Tropical fruit, skin not edible.

pau. Finished.

Pele, Madame. Legendary fire goddess of Hawaii's volcanoes.

peridot. Pronounced "peri-dot" or "peri-doe" (either is correct).

Pidgin English. Broken English mixed with Hawaiian words.

plumeria flower. The common name for this plant is frangipani. The flowers are very fragrant and frequently used in Hawaiian lei.

Plumeria flower clip art courtesy of http://www.clipartsheep.com

poi. Hawaiian staple; a starchy brown-gray paste made from the taro root, pounded, cooked, and thinned with water. Traditionally eaten with the fingers.

Poi illustration courtesy of en.wikipedia.org

pune'e. Sofa bed; couch.

saimin. Japanese noodle soup.

slippas. Pidgin English for slippers (flip flops).

Sushi. Rice wrapped in seaweed or tofu wrapper.

Tutu's Pupus. Gramma's snacks (cereal mix).

Author Profile: Nani Karol Barkley

The story of "Forever Friends" was adapted from the life of coauthor, Nani Karol Barkley. The events in the story are all true. Nani Karol was born in Honolulu, Hawaii, as an only child. At the age of ten she received from her father a doll, Poor Pitiful Pearl. That doll, along with the death of both of her parents by age thirteen, led to the inspiration for this story and to the founding in 1990 of the nonprofit agency, Toy Rescue Mission (visit www.toyrescuemission.org).

After the death of her parents, Nani moved to Tacoma, Washington, to live with her paternal grandparents. It was here she became known as "Karol". She remained in Tacoma where she later married Wesley (Tim) Barkley in 1968 and raised two daughters, Brenda and Dayna. She is now blessed with four grandchildren, Kurtis and Kristen Lunden and Kamryn and Karter Bunting. Karol retired from her thirteen-year professional career as a certified medical assistant to focus on other pursuits, not the least of which was founding and developing Toy Rescue Mission (TRM). In the course of developing the nonprofit, Karol also became an accomplished grant writer, inspirational speaker, and author (e-mail: toyresq21@gmail.com).

The impetus behind TRM grew out of Karol's love for children and a desire to help those in need. The comfort and security she derived from her Poor Pitiful Pearl doll (one of the few possessions from her childhood she was allowed to transport from her home in Hawaii to Washington) compelled her to find a means of providing other uprooted or needy children with a symbol of comfort. She turned her pastime for frequenting thrift stores into what was to become her passion, Toy Rescue Mission, a successful conduit for recycling gently used toys while providing her community and extended community with volunteer opportunities for all ages.

Karol's desire in the writing of this book is to share how God can turn tragedy into a rich and full life, just as he has done for her. One of the evidences is the success of Toy Rescue Mission and the impact it has had in the lives of so many individuals. Now retired as president of the organization, Karol is actively involved in her church (Sunset Bible Church of University Place) and community projects involving children.

Although not originally seeking to be a writer, Karol teamed up with coauthor, Donna Smeall, after much persuasion and repeated requests from her community, to tell the story behind Toy Rescue Mission.

In the future, Karol and coauthor, Donna Smeall, hope that "Forever Friends" will be the springboard to a collection of twelve books that will focus on uplifting stories of ethnic dolls from countries outside of the United States. Like Downhearted Dot, these dolls will help to tell the stories of how God's love and care can transform even the worst of situations into productive lives of hope and healing! As evidence of this impact, it is worth noting that Karol still has her original Poor Pitiful Pearl (Downhearted Dot) doll after all these years!

Author Profile: D. G. Smeall (Donna Gates-Smeall)

Although born in New London, Connecticut, Donna Gates-Smeall has chosen to make her home in the glory of Washington State's beauty. She moved from Alabama to Washington sixteen years ago when her current husband proposed. Smeall enjoys RVing full-time with her husband, Jim and their Siamese cat, Callie T. Kitty.

Smeall holds a bachelor's degree in English, (MWR emphasis) conferred by Pacific Lutheran University of Tacoma, Washington in 2005. She also holds two associate degrees, one in arts and sciences and one in communications. Her study focus has been on writing techniques for all media forms.

Smeall has, to her credit, thirty-four poetry publications, published by various organizations over the years. She started writing poetry at the age of thirteen and continued on with her creative writing, branching out into newsletter journalism with one published volume of poetry entitled "Com-PEN-di-um" published by Publish America. Other aspects of Smeall's success in writing have come in the form of awards received for her excellence in academic study in communications.

Smeall is a freelance writer employed in the pursuit of sharing inspiring stories for readers for all ages. Smeall teamed up with coauthor, Karol Barkley, when she joined Toy Rescue Mission's staff to volunteer her services as the newsletter editor. Learning of Smeall's academic background and writing achievements, Karol approached her about coauthoring a children's book that would help tell the story behind the founding of TRM and the passion that helped keep it going. The partnership proved to be a complementary fit, and with determination and dedication, Smeall and Karol have finally succeeded in achieving their first goal—the publication of this book, the first in a soon-to-be-completed collection of twelve books!

Just for fun, Donna looked up her Hawaiian name and found it to be *Kona,* meaning a leeward wind. Like the leeward wind, Donna now weaves her way down America's roads with her husband, Jim and their siamese cat, Callie as full-time RVers, seeking out new inspiring stories to write and share. Their home is where they park the wheels of their RV.

Photo Archive

The real Daddy, Mama, and Nani (Karol)

Mainland Keiki's Ohana Party Menu

Tutu's Pupus (cereal snack mix)

Fruit: pineapple, papaya, coconut, mango, and bananas

Sweet and sour piggies on toothpicks (Little Smokies dipped in sweet and sour sauce)

Lilikoi (passionfruit) juice (available at most supermarkets)

Haupia (coconut finger gelatin squares)

Hawaiian Luau clipart courtesy of http://freeclipartstore.com/

Haupia Recipe

Haupia clipart courtesy of
https://commons.wikimedia.org/wiki/File:Haupia.jpg

(Makes twenty squares)

3 c. canned coconut milk
5 ½ tbsp. cornstarch
4 ½ tbsp. sugar
1 tsp. vanilla
1/8 tsp. salt

1. Mix cornstarch, sugar, salt, and coconut milk and boil, stirring constantly until thickened. It should be free of lumps and be like thick syrup.
2. Use an electric mixer to smooth lumps, if needed.
3. Add vanilla.
4. Pour into a shallow nine-by-thirteen-inches pan. Let it cool. Refrigerate until set.
5. Cut into two-inch cubes and serve on oval leaves (cut out of green plastic plates).

Kapa prints copied from:
http://www.kapahawaii.com/hawaiian-kapa-designs-and-patterns.html

Making Homemade Kapa

Kapa is a type of cloth made from the paper-bark tree and used to make clothes in old Hawaii.

1. Cut twelve-by-twelve-inch squares from a brown paper grocery store bag. Give a square to each guest.
2. Mash the square up in your hands to form a ball.
3. Then open it up and begin rubbing it together (against itself) until the paper becomes soft and pliable, like fabric. It is now ready to be painted.
4. Using typical colors found in Hawaiian nature, brown, black, white, yellow, red, and orange, paint designs on your kapa cloth.
5. When dry, your kapa is now ready to be used as a placemat, a centerpiece or framed and hung on the wall!

Typical Hawaiian designs are zigzag lines, straight lines, dots, triangles, etc. as you see in the illustrations at left. Some designs have meanings or are interpretations of the things that Hawaiians people were accustomed to seeing in their day-to-day life such as the feathers of a bird, the bones of a fish, the teeth of a shark, and other animal parts.